Feeding

Our Feathered Friends

Feeding
Our Feathered Friends

by Dean T. Spaulding

Lerner Publications Company • Minneapolis

To my family and friends, for putting up with my hobby for all these years.

Photo Acknowledgments

Photos copyrighted to and reproduced with the permission of: Richard Day/Daybreak Imagery, pp. 6, 9, 13, 14, 24, 26, 29, 30, 34, 37, 38, 43, 47, 51, 54; Rob Curtis/The Early Birder, pp. 2, 18, 44; Kathy Adams Clark, pp. 21, 55; Dean T. Spaulding, p. 49; Perry J. Reynolds, p. 41.

Front cover photo courtesy of O'Neill and O'Neill Nature Photography
Back cover photo courtesy of Rob Curtis/The Early Birder

Page 2: A lucifer hummingbird

Library of Congress Cataloging–in–Publication Data

Spaulding, Dean T.
    Feeding our feathered friends / Dean T. Spaulding
      p. cm. — (Birder's bookshelf)
    Includes index.
    Summary: Provides step-by-step instructions on building a backyard birdfeeder and explains which birds like which kinds of food, the best times to fill feeders, and how to keep squirrels away.
    ISBN 0-8225-3175-5 (alk. paper)
    1. Bird feeders — Design and construction — Juvenile literature. [1. Bird feeders.]
I. Title. II. Series: Spaulding, Dean T. Birder's bookshelf.
    QL676.5.S658   1997
    598 — dc20   96-28585

Manufactured in the United States of America
1 2 3 4 5 6 – JR – 02 01 00 99 98 97

CONTENTS

Different birds eat different kinds of foods. American robins prefer earthworms.

Chapter 1

Welcoming Our
Feathered Friends

You are about to start an adventure—an adventure of knowledge and creativity! In this book you will learn to build bird feeders from household odds and ends. By watching birds feed in your yard, you will be able to study them more carefully, closely, and easily.

Attracting a bird or animal is not easy. It takes a lot of work and sometimes a bit of patience. To attract a bird or any wild animal to your yard, you must give it reason for coming. Food is a basic necessity for all living things. By putting out food for the birds, you're sure to attract them.

More people are feeding the birds than ever before. Did you know that one of every four homes in the United States has a bird feeder?

Before You Get Started

You don't need to go to a store and buy materials to do the projects in this book. Almost all the materials are odds and ends that we already have around the house—things that we often throw away after we're done using them. Let your family know what materials you need, so they can save them for you.

No projects in this book include Styrofoam, a type of plastic. Chemicals used to make Styrofoam can harm the ozone layer, a section of the earth's atmosphere. In addition, if not disposed of properly, Styrofoam can end up in streams, rivers, lakes, and oceans. It floats on top of the water, tricking fish and birds—they think it's food. Animals that eat Styrofoam do not live very long.

Difficulty Levels

The projects in this book are divided into three difficulty levels. *Level 1* is the easiest. You don't need a parent or teacher to help you with level-1 projects. They take only about five minutes to complete, so you'll have plenty of time afterward to watch the birds as they come and enjoy your feeders.

Level-2 projects are a little more difficult. You won't need an adult with you at all times. But you might want one within yelling distance, in case you have a question with the instructions or need a helping hand. Projects from level 2 take about 15 to 30 minutes to complete.

Blue jays often visit bird feeders.

Level-3 projects are the most difficult and take the most time. Never do a level-3 project without adult help. Your whole family might want to work on level-3 projects together.

Food for the Birds

Different kinds of birds eat different kinds of food. Some birds feed on fruit and berries, others on seeds, others on plants. Some birds, such as eagles, eat fish and other small animals. Birds that hunt small animals for food are called birds of prey. A few birds, such as vultures, eat dead and decaying animals. Birds and other animals that feed on dead animals are called scavengers. Many birds live largely on insects and larvae. Examples are flycatchers, warblers, and woodpeckers. Hummingbirds eat mostly nectar from flowers.

Most birds eat more than one kind of food. An American robin might hunt for worms on your lawn, but it won't pass up ripened berries either. Orioles will eat flying insects and tiny green worms found on the leaves of trees in spring. They might also make a trip to a homemade bird feeder to feed on a juicy slice of orange.

When most people think of bird food, they think of seeds. Birds normally gather seeds that have fallen to the ground from plants. Birds will also eat seeds from your bird feeders. Most of the feeders you'll learn to make in this book need to be filled with birdseed, though you'll also make a few feeders that hold fruit and other kinds of foods.

The kind of food a bird eats depends a lot on the shape, size, and strength of its bill, or beak. The long, thin bill of the hummingbird is just right for reaching into tube-shaped flowers to get the nectar inside. Crossbills get their name from their unusual bills, which cross at the tips. The bills are like a sharp pair of scissors. They help the crossbill cut or strip away the outer casings of cones, such as pine cones, to get at the seeds inside. Grosbeaks and cardinals have short, thick bills that they use like nutcrackers, crushing the shells of sunflower seeds. Chickadees also eat sunflower seeds, but because their bills are small and not so strong, chickadees pick open one sunflower seed at a time instead of crushing it.

You can buy birdseed at grocery stores, hardware stores, and

shops that specialize in bird feeding. Some common birdseeds are thistle, cracked corn, millet, and sunflower seeds. Some birdseed comes premixed, with several kinds of seed in one bag. If you buy premixed seed, make sure the mixture contains a lot of black oil sunflower seeds. Use a variety of different seeds in your feeders, and you'll attract a variety of birds to your yard.

How much birdseed should you use? That's a good question. Never let your feeders get empty. Small, cup-shaped feeders might need to be filled every day. Larger, tube-shaped feeders might only need filling once a week.

It's important to make sure that the birdseed you use is fresh. Often, when birdseed is old, it becomes moldy. Moldy seed is easy to spot. Throw it out immediately and never feed it to the birds. But seed can get old and still not be moldy. Here's a simple way to test a sample from a bag of birdseed to see if the seed is fresh:

1. Place a teaspoon or two of seed on a wet paper towel.
2. Cover the seed with another wet paper towel.
3. Place the paper towels and seeds on a plate. Keep the towels moist at all times—do not let them dry out.
4. Put the plate on a windowsill and check the seed in a few days.
5. If the seed has sprouted (grown shoots), then it is fresh. If the seed has not sprouted, cover it again with a wet paper towel. Continue to keep the towels moist.
6. A few days later, check the seed again. If it still hasn't sprouted, then it isn't fresh, and you shouldn't use any seed from that bag.

Look It Up!

One tool that will help you learn more about birds that come to your feeders is a field guide. Field guides are special books that help people identify different species, or specific kinds, of birds. Field guides include colored drawings or photographs of birds. They list each bird's size and point out important identifying marks. Field guides also include maps that show where different birds live at different times of the year.

Field guides to birds (as well as to other animals and plants) are available at bookstores, libraries, and stores that specialize in bird-watching. Some guides list all the birds of North America. Other guides describe birds in only the eastern or western part of the continent, or maybe just one state. Look for a field guide that applies to your region of the country.

As different birds come to your feeders, try to match them with species described in your field guide. By noting each bird's size, shape, color, and unique markings, and by comparing them with birds pictured in your field guide, you should be able to make a match. Bird identification is not easy. But with practice, your skills will improve.

Binoculars and a field guide will help you identify birds that come to your feeders.

Once You Start, Don't Stop

After you've hung up a bird feeder, it will take a few days for the birds to find it. Once birds have discovered the feeder, though, they might come to rely on you for food.

Birds are less likely to depend on you for food during the summer months. In summer, birds can usually find plenty of insects, larvae, and seeds that have fallen to the ground from plants. But in winter, the seeds you put out for our feathered friends could mean life or death for them.

To survive in winter, small birds such as black-capped chickadees must eat their body weight in food each day. Larger birds such as blue jays must eat about one-third of their body weight in food each day in winter. So if you start feeding the birds in fall, continue until spring.

What if your family decides to go on a vacation? Try to arrange for a neighbor, friend, or relative to stop by your house and fill your feeders. As a thank you present for helping, make the person one of your favorite feeders from this book.

Keep feeding the birds all winter long.

Be an Ornithologist

What we have learned about birds—how they live, where they travel, what they eat—all comes from observation and research. An ornithologist is a scientist who studies birds and their behavior. Ornithologists take careful notes while watching birds. They record their observations in notebooks.

You too can be an ornithologist. After building the feeders in this book, you can observe the birds that come to eat there. Just like an ornithologist, you can take notes about what you see and use your observations to answer questions.

Never try to get too close to the birds you're watching. Most birds will let you approach to within 30 or 40 feet. But if a bird begins to move around nervously as you approach, it's best not to go any closer. A good pair of binoculars will help you study birds from a safe distance. Better yet, stay indoors and watch the birds at your feeders through a window. You'll get a good view of the action without disturbing the birds.

Be Creative!

The projects in this book are only the beginning. As you spend more time feeding our feathered friends, you're sure to have original ideas for building different kinds of feeders. Be sure to name your creations.

Make sketches of your new feeders. If an idea looks great on paper but doesn't work when you build it, don't be discouraged. Keep working to make improvements. The solutions will come to you—and so will the birds!

Chapter 2

All-Purpose Feeders

Odds and ends often end up in the trash. Put them to good use instead. These all-purpose feeders can be filled with any kind of birdseed and will attract many kinds of birds.

Shopping Bag Feeder

I always ask for paper bags when I go to the grocery store. Somehow, though, I always end up with a pile of plastic shopping bags anyway. By making the Shopping Bag Feeder, you can recycle plastic bags.

Level: 1

Tools Needed:
scissors

Materials Needed:
plastic shopping bag
rectangular baking pan
twist-tie

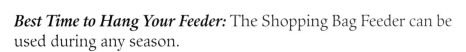

1. Put the baking pan in the plastic shopping bag.
2. Cut two large holes on opposite sides of the bag.
3. Fill the baking pan with birdseed.
4. Tie the shopping bag's handles together with a twist-tie.
5. Hang the feeder by the bag's handles.

Best Place to Hang Your Feeder: Since this feeder is made of plastic, you can hang it anywhere, from a hook on your front porch or from a tree limb in your yard. The plastic shopping bag will be a "raincoat" for the birdseed, keeping it dry.

Best Time to Hang Your Feeder: The Shopping Bag Feeder can be used during any season.

A lazuli bunting

Egg Carton Feeder

It seems like empty eggs cartons are always on hand—especially after breakfast. Gather several of them and have everyone in your family make an Egg Carton Feeder.

Level: 1

Tools Needed:
scissors

Materials Needed:
egg carton
2 pieces of wire or string
  (12 inches each)
coat hanger

1. Cut the cover off the egg carton.
2. Loop a piece of wire or string around each end of the egg carton.
3. Connect the tops of the loops to a coat hanger.
4. Hang the feeder using the coat hanger.
5. Fill the different compartments in the egg carton with different kinds of seed. Which seeds do the birds like best?

Best Place to Hang Your Feeder: This feeder doesn't have a cover. To protect it from bad weather, place it under the eaves of your roof or on a covered porch.

Best Time to Hang Your Feeder: The Egg Carton Feeder is a year-round feeder. Use it any time. Clean it between seasons by wiping it out with a wet cloth.

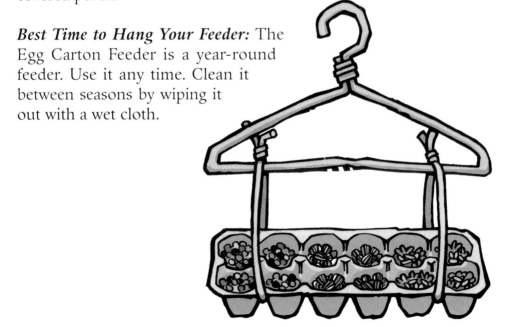

Milk Carton Feeder

When I was young, I didn't always want to drink my milk. But I drank it anyway, knowing that the sooner the milk carton was empty, the sooner I could make a Milk Carton Feeder.

Level: 2

Tools Needed:	**Materials Needed:**
scissors	½ gallon cardboard
stapler	milk carton
ruler	a few feet of string
felt-tipped marker	

1. With warm water, wash the inside of the milk carton. Let it dry.
2. Draw a 3-inch by 4-inch window on one side of the carton. Make sure that the window is at least 1 inch from the bottom of the carton.
3. Cut out the window.
4. Draw another window (the same size) on the opposite side of the carton.
5. Cut out the second window.
6. Close the spout of the milk carton and staple it shut.

A red-breasted nuthatch

7. With the end of your scissors, make a small hole through the spout.
8. Loop a piece of string through the hole and tie the ends together. Use the string to hang the feeder.
9. With your scissors, make several small slits in the bottom of the carton to serve as drainage holes.
10. Pour seed into the carton, filling it to the bottom edge of the windows.

Best Place to Hang Your Feeder: Milk cartons have a waxy coating that keeps the carton from becoming soggy with milk. So your Milk Carton Feeder won't become soggy in the rain. You can hang it anywhere.

Best Time to Hang Your Feeder: Like Chinese takeout food, there is never a bad time for this feeder. Make it and hang it all year long.

Stiff Shirt Feeder

There are many ways to recycle old clothes. When the weather is warm, many people sell old clothes at lawn sales. You can recycle old clothes and feed the birds at the same time. An old shirt makes a wonderful bird feeder. Just make sure that no one in your family is planning to wear the shirt before you use it!

Level: 2

Tools Needed:
scissors

Materials Needed:
old long-sleeved shirt,
   with a front pocket if
   possible
coat hanger
small aluminum can
4 pieces of string
   (about 6 inches each)

1. With your scissors, make three ⅛-inch slits in different places on each sleeve. Be careful not to make the slits any bigger than ⅛ inch (or all the seed will spill out).
2. Take a piece of string and tie it around the upper part of one of the shirt's sleeves—near the shoulder. Make sure that you tie the string tight.
3. Tie another piece of string around the other sleeve.
4. Fill each arm of the shirt with birdseed. You could use sunflower seed in one sleeve and thistle, cracked corn, or millet in the other.

5. After each sleeve is filled with seed, tie it closed with another piece of string (right above the cuff).

6. Put the shirt on a coat hanger and button it up, just like you would if you were hanging the shirt in your closet.

7. If the shirt has a front pocket, put an empty can in the pocket. A small soup can will work well.

8. Fill the can with another kind of birdseed. The pocket will make an extra feeding station for the birds.

9. Hang your Stiff Shirt Feeder using the hanger's hook.

Best Place to Hang Your Feeder: Hang your Stiff Shirt Feeder anywhere you like—except inside the closet!

Best Time to Hang Your Feeder: This feeder can be used in spring, summer, winter, and fall.

A tufted titmouse

Country Club Feeder

If you or anyone in your family plays tennis, this feeder is for you. After a while, tennis balls wear out and go flat. The Country Club Feeder lets you reuse them.

If you don't have any flat tennis balls around your house, visit your local tennis court. Walk around the fence. Many times, tennis players lose balls or forget to retrieve them after a game. Ask the staff of the local country club if they have any extra tennis balls.

Level: 3

Tools Needed:
scissors
serrated knife
felt-tipped marker
quarter

Materials Needed:
3 worn-out tennis balls
18-inch piece of coated
  electrical wire

1. Using your marker, trace the outline of a quarter on each of the three tennis balls.
2. Have a parent or teacher cut out the circles with a serrated knife. A heavy-duty pair of scissors will also work.
3. With the point of your scissors, make small holes on opposite ends of each tennis ball. The holes should be at right angles (90 degrees) to the cut-out circles.
4. Tie a knot at the end of the electrical wire. Thread the wire through both holes in the first tennis ball until the ball comes to rest on the knot.
5. A few inches above the ball, tie another knot in the wire. Thread another tennis ball onto the wire until the ball comes to rest at the second knot.
6. Tie another knot and thread the third ball.
7. Fill the tennis balls by pouring seed into the larger center holes.

Best Place to Hang Your Feeder: Tennis balls have a layer of rubber beneath their green or yellow "fur." This rubber will keep seed from getting wet. So you can hang your Country Club Feeder anywhere.

Best Time to Hang Your Feeder: Since your Country Club Feeder is weatherproof, you can use it year-round. You may not be able to play tennis in the winter, but that doesn't mean you can't use your Country Club Feeder.

Chickadees enjoy suet.

Chapter 3

Suet Feeders

When I was a boy, I watched my grandmother fill her bird feeders with seed. Every once in a while, she took a clump of white stuff from the freezer and placed it in a red bag that hung from the limb of a tree. I knew that woodpeckers, chickadees, and nuthatches liked whatever my grandmother put in the bag. But I never knew what the stuff was until I started feeding birds myself.

The white stuff that my grandmother put in the bag was called suet. Suet is lard, or fat, from animals. In the old days, suet was used as cooking fat. Few people cook with suet anymore. But many people use suet to feed birds.

Onion Bag Suet Feeder

The Onion Bag Suet Feeder is easy to make. You can buy suet in the meat department of your grocery store. If you don't see it on display, ask the butcher. Suet doesn't cost a lot, and it lasts a long time if stored in the freezer. If you don't use all your suet during one season, put it in the freezer and save it for next year.

Level: 1

Tools Needed:
None

Materials Needed:
1 pound of suet
small, netted onion bag
twist-tie
a few feet of string,
   fishing line, or wire

1. Place the suet in the onion bag.
2. Close the bag with the twist-tie.
3. Hang the bag using string, fishing line, or wire.

Best Place to Hang Your Feeder: Many birds will fly back and forth between your seed feeders and your suet feeder, taking a sample of each food as they go. Most birds

that eat suet are tree climbers such as woodpeckers. So it's a good idea to hang your suet feeder on or near a tree trunk.

Best Time to Hang Your Feeder: Flies, other bugs, and mold will ruin suet in hot weather. So don't use your suet feeder in summer. Put a big chunk of suet out in late fall and keep some out until spring. Suet provides birds with the extra energy they need during cold winter months.

A downy woodpecker

Soda Bottle Suet Feeder

Usually, only one bird at a time can feed at the Onion Bag Suet Feeder. With the Soda Bottle Suet Feeder, many birds can eat at once.

Level: 2

Tools Needed:
scissors
quarter
ruler

Materials Needed:
2-liter plastic soda pop
    bottle
glue
6 pieces of burlap or
    cloth (2 inches by
        2 inches)
a few feet of string
    or wire
plenty of suet

A white-breasted nuthatch might visit your suet feeders.

1. Soak the bottle for a few minutes in warm water and remove the label. Let the bottle dry.
2. With your scissors, cut the top off the bottle, about 2 inches below the neck.
3. Trace six circles at different places on the bottle, using your quarter as a guide.
4. Cut out the circles with your scissors.

5. Glue the fabric squares onto the bottle, one underneath each circle. Birds will cling to the fabric as they eat.

6. With your scissors, make a few cuts in the bottom of the bottle for drainage.

7. Cut two small holes on each side of the top of the bottle. Thread your string or wire through the holes and knot it to make a hanger.

8. Fill the bottle with suet.

Best Place to Hang Your Feeder: You can hang your Soda Bottle Suet Feeder anywhere. On or near a tree is best.

Best Time to Hang Your Feeder: Like the Onion Bag Suet Feeder, the Soda Bottle Suet Feeder should not be used in summer. Put the feeder out in fall, keeping it full of suet throughout winter and spring. Wash the feeder in summer and store it until fall.

Chapter 4

Leftover Feeders

Birds like leftovers just as much as people do. Leftover feeders are simple to make and easy to take care of. You don't even need to buy birdseed. Just remember the birds after breakfast, lunch, and dinner.

Fork Feeder

Birds will even eat leftovers off a fork! Make several Fork Feeders and hang them from a tree on your lawn.

Level: 1

Tools Needed:
scissors

Materials Needed:
plastic or metal fork
a few feet of string or
    fishing line
a piece of cloth, 1 inch
    by 1 inch
glue

1. Put glue on one side of the piece of cloth.
2. Wrap the cloth around the middle of the fork's handle.
3. Let the glue dry. Birds will grip the cloth with their feet when they eat from the feeder.
4. Tie one end of a piece of string or fishing line around the handle of the fork.
5. Tie the other end of the string or fishing line to a tree branch or metal hook in your yard.
6. You can stick just about anything on your Fork Feeder: old apple slices, a stale bagel, even French fries would make a delicious snack.

Best Place to Hang Your Feeder: Hang the Fork Feeder anywhere. It fits in the tightest spots.

Best Time to Hang Your Feeder: Use the Fork Feeder all year long.

Eggshell Snacks

Not only do recycled egg cartons make good bird feeders, but recycled eggshells make good bird food. Eggshells are rich in calcium and can be a nutritious snack for our feathered friends. The next time you or a family member eats eggs, save the shells. Put them in your feeders alongside the birdseed.

Level: 1

Tools Needed:	*Materials Needed:*
towel	eggshells

1. Wash the shells from a couple of eggs.
2. Pat the shells dry with a towel.
3. Let the shells dry overnight.
4. Crush the shells into tiny pieces with your hands.
5. Put the crushed eggshells into one of the sections of your Egg Carton Feeder or into another kind of all-purpose feeder.

A mourning dove

Stale Bread String Feeder

People often leave out stale bread for the birds—only to have dogs, squirrels, and chipmunks find the bread first. The Stale Bread String Feeder keeps bread above the ground, away from animals that can't fly.

Level: 1

Tools Needed:
scissors

Materials Needed:
a few feet of string or
    fishing line
stale bread

1. Loop the string or fishing line around the center of a piece of stale bread and tie a snug knot.
2. Loop the string or line around the bread a second time, crosswise to the first loop. Tie another knot.
3. Leave 8 to 12 inches of line for hanging the feeder.

Best Place to Hang Your Feeder: Hang your Stale Bread String Feeder anywhere. Many birds that like stale bread also like suet. So hang your Stale Bread String Feeder close to your suet feeders.

Best Time to Hang Your Feeder: Hang your Stale Bread String Feeder any time of year. As long as you have stale bread from the kitchen, the birds will enjoy eating it.

Chapter 5

Thistle-Seed Feeders

If you were a member of the finch family, thistle seed, a small black seed, would be at the top of your list of favorite foods. Pick up some thistle seed at your local birding supply store. The finches will be glad you did.

Sock Thistle Feeder

The Sock Thistle Feeder is one of my favorites. The idea came to me when I was looking at a mail-order catalog of bird feeders. One feeder was made out of a specially designed stocking and was meant to be used with thistle seed.

Looking at the picture, I thought I could make a feeder like that myself. One day, when I was putting on my shoes to go outside and fill my bird feeders, the idea came to me. It was right there on my foot—my sock!

Three American goldfinches feed at a store-bought thistle-seed feeder.

Level: 1

Tools Needed:
scissors

Materials Needed:
1 sock, any size
a few feet of string

1. Using the very tip of your scissors, *carefully* cut three or four ⅛-inch snips in different places on the sock.
2. Fill the sock with thistle seed.
3. Tie off the open end of the sock using a piece of string.
4. Hang your Sock Thistle Feeder using more string.

Best Place to Hang Your Feeder: Your Sock Thistle Feeder can be hung anywhere. Rain will not harm it. Hang it near your other

bird feeders and give the goldfinches, purple finches, and other finches a good selection of foods to choose from.

Best Time to Hang Your Feeder: Many members of the finch family look different in different seasons. American goldfinches are a good example. In summer, their yellow bodies brighten my afternoons. But when they come to my feeders in winter, they look like totally different birds. They have traded their bright yellow feathers for drab olive-colored ones. Keep your Sock Thistle Feeder out all year long so you'll be able to see this change for yourself.

Tip: If your Sock Thistle Feeder gets dirty, simply wash it. After all, it's only a sock.

Goldfinches are brightly colored in summer.

Paper Towel Thistle Feeder

Thistle seed can be a little expensive. But with the Paper Towel Thistle Feeder, not a lot of seed gets wasted.

Level: 2

Tools Needed:
scissors
ruler
pencil

Materials Needed:
cardboard tube from a
    roll of paper towels
rubber band
piece of cloth or
    plastic food wrap
a few feet of string
    or wire
pencil, pen (remove the
    inkwell), or plastic
    straw

1. Make a mark with your pencil about 3 inches from one end of the cardboard tube. (This end will be the bottom of your feeder.)
2. Make another mark opposite the first.
3. On each mark, make a tiny slit with your scissors. The slits should be no wider than ¼ inch.
4. Make pencil marks 1½ inches below the slits.
5. With your scissors, make a small hole on each of the pencil marks.
6. Take an old pencil, pen, or plastic straw and slide it through both holes—creating perches for the birds.

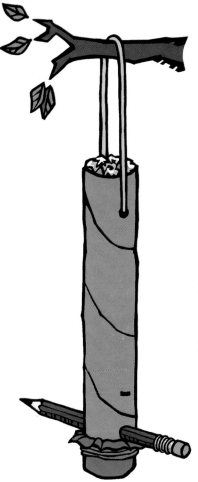

Make sure the perches are about equal in length.

7. Place the cloth or plastic wrap under the bottom of the tube. Use a rubber band to hold the cloth or plastic tightly against the tube, just below the perches.

8. Make a mark about an inch below the top of the feeder. Make another mark opposite the first.

9. Cut a small hole at each mark with your scissors.

10. Loop string or wire through the holes and tie the ends together to make a hanger.

11. Fill the tube with thistle seed. For a moment, pretend you arc a bird. Look at the slits above the perches. Can you see the thistle seed? If you can't, carefully widen the openings a little, using the point of your scissors. Step back and look again. If you can see the seed, the birds will be able to reach it without a problem.

12. To keep rain, snow, and maybe a curious bird from getting inside your feeder, wad a piece of tinfoil into a ball and stuff it into the top of the tube. The ball should fit snugly, but make sure you can grab and remove the ball when it's time to refill the feeder.

Tip: Thistle seed is very small and thin. If the slits above the perches are too big, seed will drain out. If you accidentally make a slit too big and seed does fall out, don't throw the feeder away. Place a piece of tape over the slit. Start over again with a new, smaller slit near the first.

Best Place to Hang Your Feeder: You can hang your Paper Towel Thistle Feeder just about anywhere. If you live in an area that gets a lot of rain, you might want to hang your feeder under a porch so that it stays dry.

Best Time to Hang Your Feeder: Finches will enjoy eating from this feeder all year long.

A purple finch

Chapter 6

Nectar Feeders

Nectar is sweet liquid from fruits and flowers. Here are some nectar feeders that will have the birds coming back for more.

The Six-Pack Oriole Feeder

Eight different species of orioles are found in North America. No matter where you live, orioles probably live in your area during part of the year.

Orioles love nectars—especially from oranges. Orioles that come to your Six-Pack Oriole Feeder will be sure to thank you with their hearty appetites and their bright colors.

Level: 1

Tools Needed:
scissors

Materials Needed:
plastic six-pack soda
pop rings
small orange

1. Wash and dry the rings from a six-pack of soda pop.
2. Cut an orange in half. Wedge one half into the middle of one of the plastic rings.
3. With your scissors, snip off all the extra rings but one. Hang the feeder using the one ring you didn't cut off.
4. Change the fruit in your feeder once every few weeks.

Orioles love oranges.

Best Place to Hang Your Feeder: Try to hang your oriole feeder on or near a maple, elm, or beech tree. A pair of orioles might already be nesting, or raising a family there!

Best Time to Hang Your Feeder: Spring is a good time to hang your Six-Pack Oriole Feeder. Orioles look for mates and places to build their nests in spring.

Tip: If ants find your feeder before the orioles do, put a little cooking oil on a cloth and rub it on the plastic ring.

Hummingbirds use their long, narrow bills to reach into flowers for nectar.

Hummingbird Feeder

About 15 species of hummingbirds live in North America. No matter where you live in the United States, at least one kind of hummingbird can be found there. Some areas are home to three or four species.

Hummingbirds are the smallest birds in North America. They can fly forward, backward, even upside down. They can hover in midair, which is helpful since they feed on nectar from flowers and might not find a place to perch while they're feeding.

Hummingbirds like red flowers the most. In fact, they're attracted to anything that's red. I've seen hummingbirds try to feed at a red car, a red soda pop can, and a red plastic flower on a woman's hat. Many people attract hummingbirds by planting large gardens of red flowers such as petunias, geraniums, fuchsias, and trumpet vines.

You can attract hummingbirds to your home with nothing more than a simple feeder and some nectar that you mix up in your kitchen (recipe on page 46). Making a hummingbird feeder is much easier than planting a garden. You don't even have to get your hands dirty. Here's how:

Level: 3

Tools Needed:
scissors

Materials Needed:
small salad dressing con-
    tainer
red fingernail polish or a
    piece of red ribbon
coat hanger
twist-tie

1. Wash and dry the salad dressing bottle.
2. Fold the coat hanger in half.
3. Wrap the hanger around the bottle.
4. Tie the ends of the coat hanger together with a twist-tie. The hanger holds the bottle in place.
5. With fingernail polish, paint the rim of the bottle red, or tie a red ribbon around the bottleneck. (If you use nail polish, be sure to let it dry before hanging the feeder.)
6. Hang the feeder by the hook of the coat hanger. Make sure the bottle is tilted slightly upward, so the nectar doesn't pour out.

Hummingbird Nectar

Hummingbirds beat their wings hundreds of times per second. This motion not only makes a "humming" sound, it also takes a lot of energy. Hummingbirds must eat often—every 15 minutes—to stay alive. Though hummingbirds normally feed on nectar from flowers, you can make a different kind of nectar for your hummingbird feeder.

Tools Needed:	*Materials Needed:*
spoon	1 cup sugar
measuring cup	4 cups water

1. In a bowl, mix 1 cup of sugar into 4 cups of water.
2. Stir the mixture well with a spoon. Add a little extra sugar (½ cup) to your first batch of nectar. After the hummingbirds have found your feeder, you can make more nectar with the normal recipe.
3. Boil the mixture on the stove (have a parent help you). Let the mixture cool a bit. Then place it in the refrigerator for a while.
4. Carefully pour the homemade nectar into the feeder.

Best Place to Hang Your Feeder: A garden is a great place to hang your feeder. You might want to tie a piece of string or fishing line to the coat hanger so that you can hang your feeder low and close to some flowers.

Best Time to Hang Your Feeder: People who live in warm areas see hummingbirds all year long. If you live in a place where it

gets cold and snows in the winter, you will only be able to feed hummingbirds from spring until fall.

Tips: If there are no red flowers in your yard, tie some red ribbons to the hanger. Make some more hummingbird feeders and decorate them with ribbons of different colors. Which feeders do the hummingbirds like most? Do they really like red best?

Hummingbirds won't be the only ones attracted to your feeder. Ants will also be interested. If ants become a problem, rub a little cooking oil on the coat hanger.

Cleaning: During summer, clean your feeder every week. During spring and fall, clean your feeder every other week. Wash it with hot water and a drop of vinegar. Make sure to rinse all the cleaning solution out of the bottle before refilling it with nectar.

Never use old nectar. Make a fresh batch each time you clean out the feeder. Refill the feeder to the very top of the bottle. A clean, full feeder will attract lots of hummingbirds.

Red flowers attract hummingbirds.

Chapter 7

Extras

Squirrel Baffle

If you've ever watched a squirrel gather nuts for winter, you've probably noticed how hard these animals work. Squirrels are very industrious when it comes to finding food—especially the food inside your bird feeders.

Bird feeders and squirrels do not mix. Squirrels can destroy a bird feeder in minutes, chewing it with their sharp teeth. You can "squirrelproof" a bird feeder by making a squirrel baffle.

Level: 1

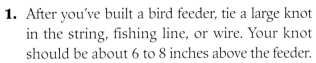

Tools Needed:
scissors

Materials Needed:
a plastic lid (6 to 8 inches across) from a large tub of whipped cream or margarine

1. After you've built a bird feeder, tie a large knot in the string, fishing line, or wire. Your knot should be about 6 to 8 inches above the feeder.
2. With your scissors, make a ⅛-inch slit in the middle of the plastic lid.
3. Slide the lid down the string, line, or wire until it rests on the knot.
4. Don't be alarmed if the baffle tips back and forth—it's supposed to. The unsteadiness of the baffle keeps squirrels from climbing all the way down the line and onto your feeder.

Tip: Baffles don't always work. Squirrels are smart animals, and they will even jump from far-off trees to get at bird feeders. If squirrels become a big problem, try adding two squirrel baffles to your feeders instead of just one.

Keeping squirrels away from bird feeders can be difficult.

Natural Sunflower Feeder

This feeder cannot be built with odds and ends. It must be *grown* instead. People sometimes spill seed when they're filling feeders, or birds accidentally drop seeds to the ground. Eventually, a few of these seeds work their way into the soil and sprout.

Most commercial birdseed contains some sunflower seeds, and sunflowers sometimes sprout beneath bird feeders. This event doesn't have to happen by accident. You can create Natural Sunflower Feeders yourself!

Level: 1

Tools Needed:
small shovel or spade

Materials Needed:
potting soil
clay, tin, or plastic pot
(with drainage holes)
5 or 6 fresh sunflower
seeds from a bag
of birdseed

1. Fill the pot with soil to about 2 inches from the top.
2. Place five or six sunflower seeds on top of the soil.
3. Cover the seeds with another inch of soil and pat gently.
4. Put the pot on your porch or patio.
5. Water the soil whenever it's dry.

Within a week or so, sprouts will appear. It will take several months, but the sprouts will eventually turn into tall plants with thick stocks and big, yellow flowers.

Sunflowers love sunlight—that's how they got their name. Notice in the morning how the sunflowers' yellow faces point east. Then, as the sun moves west, so do the flowers.

After a while, the sunflowers' faces will start to dry up. You'll soon find sunflower seeds inside the faces of the flowers. The birds will find them too!

Best Place to Put Your Feeder: Place the pot of sunflowers on the ground near your other bird feeders. Birds will quickly find and enjoy the seeds.

Best Time to Make Your Feeder: Since sunflowers grow only in warm weather, make your feeder in spring and leave it out all summer.

Bird Savers

There is probably no more comfortable place for bird-watching than the indoors. Usually, watching birds through a window lets you take a close look at the birds without frightening or harming them.

Sadly, windows do sometimes harm birds. Birds such as northern cardinals and American robins sometimes fly into windows. More than 100 million birds are killed this way each year.

It's usually not because the bird can't see the window. The bird sees its *reflection* in the window and—not realizing the image is a reflection—flies toward it, trying to scare the "intruding" bird off.

When feeding birds at our homes, it's important to make our windows safe for the birds we invite. "Bird savers" are stickers on windows that interfere with reflections. When bird savers are attached to a window, birds are less likely to see their own images and fly toward them.

Level: 1

Tools Needed:

scissors

pencil

Materials Needed:

black construction
  paper

tracing paper

tape

1. Using tracing paper, copy the outline of a falcon.
2. Tape the tracing paper to the construction paper.
3. Cut around the outline, cutting the falcon shape out of the construction paper.
4. Tape the paper falcon to the inside of your window. If the window is large, make several bird savers and place them all around the window.

Tip: Your bird savers don't have to be falcon-shaped. Any design will work: tulips, hearts, triangles, or circles. All of these will keep birds away from your windows.

GLOSSARY

binoculars: optical devices that magnify, or enlarge, images. Bird-watchers use binoculars to get a good view of birds from a distance.

field guide: a book that shows pictures of different birds and describes their characteristics. Field guides help people identify different species of birds.

nesting: the process of building a nest, laying eggs, and raising young birds

ornithologist: a scientist who studies birds

species: a specific kind of animal within a larger group of similar animals

Index

About the Author

Dean T. Spaulding is an environmental journalist and wildlife photographer. His work has appeared in *Audubon, Wild Bird, Birder's World,* and other publications. He is a member and former president of the Adirondack High Peaks Audubon Society and lives in upstate New York.

John Monroe

For more information:
National Audubon Society
700 Broadway
New York, NY 10003
212-979-3000